NIKKI ILES
JAZZ IN SPRINGTIME
9 pieces for jazz piano

Contents

MUSIC DEPARTMENT

OXFORD
UNIVERSITY PRESS

This collection © Oxford University Press 2013
Nikki Iles has asserted her right under the Copyright, Designs and patents Act, 1988, to be identified as the Author of these works

ISBN 978–0–19–339155–0

Credits

Cover illustration by Tony Stephenson © Oxford University Press
Artist photo by Hugh Byrne

The Jazz in Springtime CD, featuring Nikki Iles, was recorded at
Red Gables Facilities, Greenford, on 12 December 2012
Engineered and co-produced by Ken Blair, BMP The Sound Recording Company

Music origination by Katie Johnston
Printed in Great Britain on acid-free paper by Halstan & Co. Ltd, Amersham, Bucks.

Honeysuckle Rose

words by ANDY RAZAF
music by THOMAS 'FATS' WALLER
arr. Nikki Iles

4

to Coda ⊕

D.S. al Coda   ⊕ CODA

swing hard

inspired by Art Tatum

May Song

trad. English
arr. Nikki Iles

inspired by Iain Ballamy

I've got the world on a string

words by TED KOEHLER
music by HAROLD ARLEN
arr. Nikki Iles

Medium swing ♩ = 108

to Coda ⊕

D.S. al Coda   ⊕ **CODA**

inspired by Oscar Peterson

Mwanzo

NIKKI ILES

D.S. al Coda

⊕ **CODA**

Majestically (slower)

Ped. _____

8vb

inspired by Abdullah Ibrahim

It might as well be Spring

words by OSCAR HAMMERSTEIN
music by RICHARD RODGERS
arr. Nikki Iles

Bright samba ♩ = 88

D.S. al Coda $\oplus$ **CODA**

inspired by Stan Getz

* Play bracketed G first time only.

April in Paris

words by E. Y. HARBURG
music by VERNON DUKE
arr. Nikki Iles

inspired by Count Basie

Up on the Hill

NIKKI ILES

inspired by Mark Lockheart

Spring can really hang you up the most

words by FRAN LANDESMAN
music by TOMMY WOLF
arr. Nikki Iles

inspired by Ella Fitzgerald

Flores

NIKKI ILES

Gentle, loping swing ♩ = 116

inspired by Miles Davis and Chick Corea